Talk Poetry

Other titles from Miami University Press

Poetry Series

General Editor: James Reiss

The Bridge of Sighs	Steve Orlen
People Live, They Have Lives	Hugh Seidman
This Perfect Life	Kate Knapp Johnson
The Dirt	Nance Van Winckel
Moon Go Away, I Don't Love You No More	Jim Simmerman
Selected Poems: 1965–1995	Hugh Seidman
Neither World	Ralph Angel
Now	Judith Baumel
Long Distance	Aleda Shirley
What Wind Will Do	Debra Bruce
Kisses	Steve Orlen
Brilliant Windows	Larry Kramer
After A Spell	Nance Van Winckel
Kingdom Come	Jim Simmerman
Dark Summer	Molly Bendall
The Disappearing Town	John Drury
Wind Somewhere, and Shade	Kate Knapp Johnson
The Printer's Error	Aaron Fogel
Gender Studies	Jeffrey Skinner
Ariadne's Island	Molly Bendall
Burning the Aspern Papers	John Drury
Beside Ourselves	Nance Van Winckel

General Editor: Keith Tuma

Rainbow Darkness: an anthology of African-American poetry, edited by Keith Tuma

Fiction Series

Edited by the Creative Writing Faculty of Miami University

Mayor of the Roses	Marianne Villanueva
The Waiting Room	Albert Sgambati

Talk Poetry

By Mairéad Byrne

Miami University Press
Oxford, Ohio

Library of Congress Cataloging-in-Publication Data

Byrne, Mairéad.
 Talk Poetry / by Mairéad Byrne.
   p. cm. -- (The Miami University Press poetry series)
 ISBN 1-881163-49-0
 I. Title.
PR6052.Y678T36 2007
821'.92--dc22

Acknowledgements

Many thanks to the editors of the following publications in which the poems listed were first published:

5 AM: "Personal Insurance"
American Poetry Review: "What Is A Cell Phone?"
Black Clock: "Can You Die Of Eating Pancakes" "Trapeze Act"
Carve: "From The Air," "Rose-Colored Spectacles"
Coconut: "Metaphor Recoil," "State Pathologist," "The Letter"
Dead Horse Review: "News," "Parking"
Denver Quarterly: "The Russian Week"
Effing Magazine: "Revision" (titled "Art"), "Shingle," "The New Sponge"
Famous Reporter: "Forward Planning"
Fascicle: "Circus," "Duplicates," "I Went To The Doctor," "We Went To The Moon"
Free Verse: "Emissary," "Family Photos," "Slippage"
Intercapillary Space: "Climbing The Stairs," "Music," "That *West End Blues* Syndrome"
Lit: "America"
Margin: "Personal Insurance"
Masthead: "The Russian Week"
MiPOesias: "Traditional Pot"
Natural Bridge: "The Pressure"
Ocho: "Getting To Swansea"

Pavement Saw: "Division Of Labor," "I Went To The Gym"
RealPoetik: "Drinking My Poem," "The Important Looking Men"
Small Town: "The Tired Terrorist," "The Wind That Shakes The Barley"

"Chiasmus" was collected in *Vivas* (Wild Honey Press 2005). "Personal Insurance" and "The Russian Week" were collected in *Kalends* (Belladonna* 2005). "I Went To The Doctor" is reprinted in *Best of Irish Poetry 2007* (Munster Literature Centre, 2006). "Circus" and "Personal Insurance" are included in *Not for Mothers Only: Contemporary Poets on Child-Getting and Child-Rearing* (Fence Books 2007).

"Drinking My Poem" and "What Is A Cell Phone" were broadcast on National Public Radio's *Open Source*, June 15, 2006. "The New Sponge" was broadcast on miPOradio's *The Goodnight Show*, June 28, 2006.

to poetry

Contents

I am for an art…that is heavy and coarse and blunt and sweet and stupid as life itself.

— Claes Oldenburg

AMERICA

America is just the greatest man. We got all this space & democracy & everything & just the greatest music. Like Chuck Berry & Buddy Holly & Elvis & Bob Dylan & Bob Marley & Van Morrison & The Beatles & Vivaldi & everything. I mean how cool is that. And poets— look at what's her face Anne Bradstreet & Emily Dickins & Charles Dickinson & Walt Whitman—*WE LOVE YOU WALTER*—& Yeats & Keats & all those dudes & Langston Hughes & RUMI! This is the *GREATEST* country! *I LOVE IT! DON'T YOU JUST LOVE IT? YOU GOTTA LOVE IT!* We got *ICE-SKATERS!* We bust the *ATOM!* We got *CONIFERS!* We were the *FIRST* in space! We got the *GOBI DESERT!* We got *MONGOLIA!* And *NIAGARA!* And the *GRAND CANYON!* And *THE PYRAMIDS!* You're not going to catch me saying civilization began with the *Mayflower!* None of that shit—I mean how did those guys *BUILD* those things. *THE PYRAMIDS.* I mean people still don't understand the physics of it. They had to had rollers or something. No, King Tut is as American as anyone in my book. As American as Abe Lincoln. Did you know they had *SLAVES* back then? Isn't that the weirdest?? Hey pass me that snow globe will you. *YEAH!*

BAKING SODA

Baking soda is good for just about everything. I think we should try it in the War Against Terrorism. I heard a guy on the radio, William Odum, who used to be a General in the U.S. Army. He said you couldn't have a War Against Terrorism. Terrorism isn't an enemy. It's a strategy. *It's about as sensible to say we declare war on night attacks and expect we're going to win that war.* That's what Odom said. The *NPR* headline said: *General Odum names the problem.* Well I'm naming the solution: *Baking Soda. Solutions for:* My Home. My Family. My Body. *For the Bathroom.* Laundry Room. Garage. Family Room. Bedroom. Nursery. Outside. Playroom. Kitchen. *As an Antacid.* Cat Litter Deodorizer. Chlorine Bleach Booster. Camping Necessity. Deodorant. Detergent Booster. Hand Cleanser. Oral Appliance Soak. Refreshing Bath Soak. Soothing Foot Soak. *For Cleaning Baby Equipment.* Cleaning Baby Toys. Cleaning Bathroom Floors. Cleaning Batteries. Cleaning Brushes and Combs. Cleaning Cars. Cleaning Grills. Cleaning Lawn Furniture. Extinguishing Fires. *For Deodorizing Cars.* Deodorizing Drains. Deodorizing Camper Water Tanks. Deodorizing Musty Towels. Deodorizing Recyclables. Deodorizing Wastebaskets. *For Baby Spills on Carpet.* Carpet Spills. Dry Baths for Dogs. Facial Scrub and Body Exfoliant. Family-Safe Cleaning. Hair Care. Hand-Washing Dishes and Pots and Pans. Head-to-Toe Personal Care. Liquid Laundry. Loving Your Pets Not Their Odors. Microwave Cleaning. Mouth Cleaning. Mouth Freshening. Outdoor Fun. Piled-High Laundry. Pool Care.

Septic Care. Shower Curtains. Skin Care. Surface-Safe Cleaning. Upholstery Spills. *To Clean Baby Combs.* Clean and Deodorize Plastic Containers. Clean and Deodorize Lunch Boxes. Clean and Freshen Sports Gear. Clean Furniture. Clean Pet Toys. Clean Pool Toys. Clean Walls. Clean Up Your Mouth. *Deodorize and Clean Dishwashers.* Deodorize Baby Bottles. Deodorize Car Ashtrays. Deodorize Diaper Pails. Deodorize Drains & Garbage Disposals. Deodorize Garbage Cans. Deodorize Gym Bags. Deodorize Pet Bedding. Deodorize Retainers. Deodorize Sneakers. Deodorize Your Wash. *Freshen Ashtrays.* Freshen Closets. Freshen and Deodorize Carpets. Freshen Stuffed Animals. Freshen and Deodorize Upholstery. Freshen Towels and Sheets. *Gently Clean and Freshen Baby's Laundry. Remove Oil and Grease Stains.* Or *Just for Kids.* That about covers it. *Baking Soda*: It's a substance. It's a solution. It's a strategy. Yeah, *Arm & Hammer.* Go figure.

Can You Die Of Eating Pancakes

After my hard week's work I decided to make myself a pancake. It was a difficult commitment because I do like my granola. I had to go on a 70-minute drive & take a stiff walk on a breezy beach to brood about it. In the end I decided to put granola *into* the pancake. It was a *win-win* situation. Happily I set about my task. I remembered a pancake in Olympia Washington once which came with fruit. I cut up a serendipitous half-apple I found in the fridge & threw it in. I was frying this pancake with butter so you can imagine the effect on the apple & how delicious it all smelled. I had to go out of the house (it was cold) & come back in just to truly appreciate the aroma. Ever notice that the only time you *really* get to smell your house's smell is when you come in from outside? I used to think a certain smell was peculiar to Chinese houses until I started coming into my own house after cooking rice. The pancake, when done, was stupendous. It was actually more of a collection of pancakes. It was a pancake in the sense that Providence is a city. Sort of a cluster of pancakelets, each with the integrity & rights of a pancake, of course, especially the right to collect taxes. And no doubt there was one quintessential pancake in there which was the definitive pancake which gave the Providence *gestalt* to the lot of them. Anyhoo (never said that before) it was very high & crumbly. Very complex in its parts. It looked like a lethal weapon—or the results of one. I put lemon on it & maple syrup & set to. I'm still eating it. I'm going to be eating it a very long time. If I die, consider this my 5 lb accidental suicide note.

Chiasmus

When you marry & divorce your dreams get mixed up. You wanted an over-stuffed leather living room set and next thing you know you're heading an expedition to the South Pole *and* making a pretty good fist of it. There you are on top of the Ross Ice Shelf in the depths of winter hauling supplies to base camp, enduring 25-mile winds and a record low of -64°F with a wind-chill equivalent of -2800°F, watching the sun come up on the horizon for the first time in months when it hits you right between your frost-rimed but piercing eyes: *Wasn't it X's dream to lead an expedition to Antarctica? What am I doing here? How did this happen? How did I inherit his dream?* Meanwhile X is in Cardi's meditating on a handsome cognac top grain leather living room set with dark wood accent trim and dimpled plush back, cushioned and sectioned vertically for style and comfort, wondering if it might perhaps be more pleasing in chocolate or burgundy, harvesting his own ecstasy.

CIRCUS

There's so much emphasis on the individual we forget how much a single person is actually a double. For a start, we are symmetrical: 2 eyes, 2 nostrils, 2 lips with two halves in each one. Our 32 teeth can be divided in two so many ways they deserve a poem of their own. And, taking a bird's eye view—2 hemispheres in the brain. The story goes all the way down: 2 shoulders, 2 arms, 2 lungs, 2 kidneys, 2 testicles, 2 ovaries, 2 bums, each one divided in two, 2 knees, 2 legs, 2 feet. We are actually really 2 people in one. And what do we do? We pair up. We get married, shackled, whatever. Why we do this I do not know. We are already getting quite enough action being 2 people in one but whatever. We have to have an outside person too, who is also more 2 persons than one. It gets complex. Now you have a 2 X 4. Kids arrive. Each kid adds 2 to the mix. Sometimes there's twins. Pretty soon you have chaos masquerading as a family. I'm thinking of Ben Franklin. Now Ben was the 15th child out of a total of 17 born to his mother. This figure may or may not include 2 children who died. The numbers are staggering. I'm thinking of Mrs. Franklin. This is a woman or, to my way of thinking, practically 2 women, who had 17 or 19 children proceed through her, i.e., 34 or 38, in addition to providing accommodation for the regular visits of Mr. Franklin. This is not a woman. This is a pomegranate. This is the fabled village it takes to raise a child. Mrs. Franklin herself was the green on which the townspeople cavorted. Is it any wonder we thought of *mitosis* and *meiosis* and all that. It's written all over us. How do you end something like this? It never ends.

CITY RITUAL #29

In New England we had this ritual on November 1 where we said goodbye to the sidewalk.

The Goodbye Sidewalk Ritual. We would strew flour on the sidewalk, strew sugar. Sometimes milk.

Certain items could be laid down first: coins, cut grass, maybe a popsicle stick.

Of course sometimes it snowed before November 1, before we could do *The Goodbye Sidewalk Ritual.*

We didn't do it those years. You were aware you mightn't see the sidewalk for oh, it could be two three months.

There really should have been a kerbside ritual because kerbs were the one thing you could be sure would disappear in New England winters; I mean you could not park a car without leaving it in the middle of the street practically.

We had one other ritual with dripping taps we did a little later in the year.

The Dripping Taps Ritual.

My grandmother wrote a famous song about it. *The Dripping Taps Song.*

Climbing The Stairs

I was finding it a bit tedious climbing the stairs so I decided to up the ante. *First:* Wash the stairs. *Next:* Lay squares of paper towel down. *Then:* Move up & down the stairs stepping only on the squares of paper towel. *Rationale:* My slippers tend to leave marks on the wet steps. *Effect:* Increased difficulty climbing stairs, which action now requires tri-partite effort a) almost vertical hoisting of the legs, with b) frantic whole-body follow-through, propelled by c) pumping action of right arm against banister; with d) descent involving a domino-effect toppling, always in danger of skidding off the paper towel & the tread, always in danger of plunging straight down the stairwell like a bucket in a well. Going up & down the stairs is much harder than before, & also much more unusual. Going up is more like ice-climbing. Coming down is more like bungee-jumping. I have started going around the whole house like this. I have put squares of paper towel down in all the rooms & halls so that I can lurch around like Frankenstein, having close encounters with the floors & walls. The house has shrunk & I have grown huge, like a monstrous erection, mindless yet programmed to seek. Full report to follow.

Degrees

What happens if you receive someone else's PhD? I'm serious. People always say: *And then I went for my PhD* or *I got my PhD at Walla-Walla University* but what if you got someone else's by mistake. You wouldn't be able to understand a word of it. It would be so embarrassing. You'd have to say, *And then I got Doug Thomsen's PhD*, or whoever's name was embossed in gold on it. Say it was an MFA! And it still wasn't yours. You'd be stuck saying *And then, aw, then, aw, well then I got this MFA see, I was going for my PhD but I got this, this is what they gave me, it's poetry, prose poetry I think, yaw*. I don't know, there sure are a lot of problems in life. Not least of which is: If you have Tiny Bludgeon's MFA, who the hell has your PhD???? Probably the same motherfucker who has your eyes, your nose, your smile, your ways: THAT CANNIBAL.

Division Of Labor

When a person is throwing up you cannot help in the throw-up operation. You can pat the back, you can soothe, you can ferry basins back & forth. But essentially the person will throw up with or without you. It is just not your job.

Driving is not your job unless you are driving. There is no point leaning forward tense & hawk-like or swaying your body as the car rounds the bend as if you were a pillion passenger on a bike, another situation over which you have no control. You cannot steer the car with good vibes or vigilance, no matter how intense.

You cannot help an alcoholic. Except in the ordinary ways you can help anyone. Like sewing on a button. People do what they do. Sometimes it is beautiful.

The next time someone says to you: *I don't think I want to be with you anymore*, you say *Here is your hat*. When someone walks away their job is walking away. There's no by-product you can pluck like cotton to gather them back. Your job is looking after your old chum, yourself. Now you get to talk to the driver & say what to do. Now you get to say *One glass is enough my friend* & nod in agreement.

Throw-up is an interesting example though. Even if you are the person throwing up, it's still not really your job.

DRINKING MY POEM

I was gloomy all through the paella & the paella was beautiful: a vision of shellfish & chicken nestled on succulent rice. It tasted as good as it looked & looked as good as it tasted & there was texture too. You could have worn this paella as an Easter bonnet in Cannes or Antibes or even somewhere singular like Madrid. But I was thinking of racism, of poverty, of American cities & public schools. I tried to talk about it but just got gloomier & made everyone else gloomy too. It was one of those glooms like a shroud: you couldn't see beyond it. I see a little girl crossing the street by herself. *Gloom.* I see a small boy walking very slowly to school. *Gloom.* I hear a teacher screeching & shaming. *On & on & on & on.* I see the little kids taking it. *Gloom upon gloom.* I see a bunch of white people at a meeting in a room saying what they want & how they deserve it & how they're going to go about getting it. *Are these my people? Who are my people?* First I was confused & now this inarticulate yet communicable gloom. So I'm gloomy as I pick at nuts & little crunchy things that look like nuts & other crunchy things that look like banana slices. Gloomy through excellent salad with shaved cheese. Gloomy through chocolate mousse surrounded by fat blackberries & sliced strawberries: another vision & explosion of texture & taste. Gloomy when I accept from Lisa's hand—the same hand that laid a dish of shiny black olives on the burnished orange cloth & raised still furled roses around lilies in a tall vase on a low table in the other room—in a fluted green cup, coffee. It is rich, black & very strong. And my gloom is gone.

DUPLICATES

Another fantastic idea is—*duplicates.* It's fine to have one desk-lamp say that you carry from room to room. But imagine having a desk-lamp on your desk, a desk lamp on your other desk, a desk-lamp on your bedside table, and a floor lamp even by the couch. Can you see how incredible that could be? Instead of plugging out the one desk-lamp you have and bringing it here & there & up & down the stairs & plugging it in & out you would simply go to wherever you wished to read etc and turn the already present lamp on. I have tried this myself at home so I'm not just speaking speculatively. It has revolutionized my life. There's still one glitch in that I put one of the new desk-lamps on my daughter's desk. My daughter is at college. Meanwhile I'm soldiering on with my old bedside lamp which has to be plugged in & out because the on/off switch is broken. I decided to borrow my daughter's desk-lamp when she was away. The first time I used it I couldn't believe it! There I was bending down to plug in the sucker as usual when it hit me: *Not necessary!!!!!* Now whenever I hear she's coming home I just swiftly switch lamps. In a sense it's almost as if the lamp has been standing quietly on her desk all the time, waiting for the touch of her white hand. There's something very restful about that.

EMISSARY

After 11 years an emissary came from my country. *We missed you* he said. After all these years. He spoke about how things had changed: The embargo was lifted. All the figures were up: Employment, wages, life expectancy. Elections were being held. We met in the library, the largest room in my house. As he spoke I paced back & forth. Recalling those high hard days. Then 11 years. So many others had gone longer with no word, no call. For some, there was no more country. They had gone. They had ceased to exist for their country. Their country ceased to exist for them perhaps. And then one day ceased to exist at all, for anyone. I wondered what he wanted. What was the purpose of his visit, so to speak. He spoke about investment, education, a democratic reconciliation of differences. If I were a fiction writer I could take it from there. I could give you an explanation, a plot, a narrative. But I am a poet. I looked at his hands holding the glass, the intense black of the trim on his coat. I listened to his voice crumbling into dusk & thought about what it was like.

Family Photos

In our house we didn't have a camera. We liked photos though and posed for them at every opportunity. We didn't have a television or much in the way of music except a few Clancy Brothers records & a Leonard Cohen LP. On Sunday afternoons we liked to line up on the couch, and behind the couch, and smile like hell. There were eight children in our family. We didn't use the living room much. But we liked to dress up & grin. There was a piano. Sometimes my younger sister, who got lessons, would sit on the piano stool, and holding her hands suspended somewhat claw-like above the keys, would swivel round her head at a 90°angle to her stalwart body, her face full of mischief & intent. That was fun, though not so much for us. We piled into the tub, four or five of us, and, all facing forward, went mad with glee. After a good meal, or even before it—my mother at the roasting tin basting the turkey, the birthday candles lit and one little set of cheeks in profile swelling to blow—we liked to put our elbows on the table & beam. Parts of our house were black & white; parts were colored. My father was in charge. As far as groupings were concerned, he was the magnet, we were the metal filings. I don't know how we ever got anything done in our house, we spent so much time face-forward, grinning to beat the band.

FIGURES

I used to be 4 years younger than my husband then he left me with 2 children & I got 7 years older very quick. Two years went by. I was 11 years older then. He stayed the same age, always 30, possibly even younger. In no time, I was 20 years older than him & hurtling towards old age. Even the children began to age. They were small & wrinkled, older than their own father. His skin was baby-smooth, his brown hair rising like a stack above their wilting heads—or like a vividly brushed dun & purple mountain range ringing the horizon in the pan of which, somewhere, they tottered.

Forward Planning

I had a bit of time Sunday so I ate all my breakfasts for the week. I really like breakfast. It's probably my favorite meal. I think I would be quite happy eating breakfast at every meal. Given the range of breakfasts throughout human culture this would be no hardship. I like most of them (within reason) but maybe not so much Dutch (though I'm sure it's very good for you). [Consider Irish breakfasts: wouldn't they serve very handsomely as Christmas dinners?]. Sunday I had quite a spread: A scone and a half as per usual ration (one raisin, half blueberry); granola (raspberry) with warm milk, very nice; oatmeal in case it was cold on Tuesday; granola with warm milk (snow forecast); fresh roll & honey (yummy); a scone and a half (one blueberry plus one half raisin thus evening the score); pancakes; which brings me back to Sunday again, when I do not anticipate being short of time and so can breakfast in the traditional way in addition to reviewing & fine-tuning the plan. I felt I made good decisions and as always enjoyed my breakfast(s). Round Wednesday though I started to get distinctly peckish. Not only that—depressed. I was obliged to institute very early lunches, composed mainly of breakfast foods. One interesting side-effect of all this is that I now eat four square meals a day: one on Sunday and the other three on the day itself. Planning can increase your appetite it seems, though no doubt efficiency burns calories so it balances out. And there's another thing: The square meal. Has anyone ever tried to do something more ergonomic with that?

From The Air

I see the city's pain map. It's not as I thought. Yes, great sections are hatched with scribbled oils, scored deep, but bold suns shine there too, like rude billiard balls, & there are thousands of them, insufficiently camouflaged.

And of course the hospitals, the schools, the prisons, the police stations are plunged—but not in total darkness, not quite. Even the Family Court is not completely guttered out.

And the burnished shores of the East Side, descending in terraces, are tarnished too. Nothing has edges. Nothing is free of dusk or gold. The whole city is a scattered highway: incessant gold orbs forced into black air & roped to a permanently repressed scream.

Only the cemeteries are unvariegated, slick spills of milky greyness, pulsing faintly. *Like a fledgeling's throat.*

Getting To Swansea

All day I've been trying to figure out how to get to Swansea, or Cardiff. Or Bristol or Fishguard or Pembroke. Or Birmingham. Or Gatwick or Heathrow or Luton or Oxford. Or Dublin or Shannon or Rosslare or Cork. Depending on buses or trains or ferries or planes or maybe a rental—the M4 & driving on the left side of the road. Or time or connections or childcare or Spring Break or schedules timetables or fares. The grand pincer movement of Shannon or Dublin (then Limerick & Cork to Swansea or Dublin to Rosslare to Fishguard then Swansea) by Aer Lingus Bus Éireann to Cork Ringaskiddy then Swansea Cork Ferries with bag baggage & daughter (twice price with daughter but tight time without) or Aercoach Dublin Bus Iarnród Éireann Stena Sealink to Fishguard no taxis at Fishguard no ticket office—bus stop on main road opposite station. To Swansea? (I was thinking of writing to Harvard to say *what's your plan???*). Or Pembroke—no taxis at Pembroke no ticket office bus station one mile from the boat dock, stop outside station. To Swansea? (or Swansea or Anglesea saying *can you advise*????), or Mumbles or Gower. Or Aer Lingus or Ryanair to Birmingham or Bristol or Cardiff & buses from Digbeth or New Street or Cardiff International or Bristol to Swansea. Or rather British Air or Virgin to Heathrow or Gatwick or Luton & National Express Coach from Heathrow Central or Terminals 1, 2, 3, 4, or Gatwick South Term or North Term to Swansea. Or Heathrow Connect or Express (depending on terminal) to Paddington.

Or Gatwick Express to Victoria then tube to Great Western to Swansea. I'm not sure about Luton. And RIPTA of course & Bonanza to Logan or Boston from Providence (or MBTA to South Station, Silver Line to airport) solid in each case & in reverse too so many steps up & steps down & bridges & small aisles & small seats & small bathrooms & lurching & heaving & holding a small hand & staircases & corridors & escalators & elevators & moving walkways & glass doors expectant faces empty spaces & sidewalks & fumes complex articulation of distance relentless connection of synapse all w/ sd luggage & backwards & forwards & you know I haven't thought of England for years—or Scotland or Wales but mostly not England & now—all day long—nothing but London & Bristol or Cardiff & getting to Swansea in March.

Global Hastening

I don't know what happened to May. It disappeared in a blur of rain & grading. One minute it was May 1st. Now it's May 19th. Everything's whizzing by. When I was young summer lasted all year. It was like the ocean. Amber waves of grain rolling way off to the horizon. Now it's like *zzzpptt!* As soon as it's Monday it's Friday. Months are like weekends. You make a note to do something & 3 years later it's done. There's no point in looking forward to anything. I understand that as you get older time speeds up. But this is surreal. Everyone's hit. And it's not just a horizontal thing. It's vertical too. My daughter says *I can't BELIEVE freshman year is almost over.* My 9-year old confides to her friends *Time flies.* Babies go *bye bye bye bye.* And they can't even talk. What's happening? The temporal caps are melting. This one's for Mr. President.

A Hive Of Home

I am unreasonably fond of home. There should be some word like *uxorious* to describe how I am about home (I've always wanted to meet a *uxorious* man, haven't you?). Now that I'm back at work I have no option but to have homes everywhere. I have a home in the 8th floor bathroom of the Design Center. I have a home in the 2nd floor Ladies in Carr House. I have a holiday home in the Men's Restroom next door to my office. Bathrooms make excellent homes & I have them all over campus & indeed all over Providence, e.g., Borders, the Providence Place Mall, the Brown Book Store. All the libraries. Libraries are *de facto* homes. Bookstores are hotels. Hotels are homes though I don't usually stay in them in Providence. A bus can be a good home. Even your own seat at a meeting or reading can be home. Or the third seat in the seventh row in the movie theatre. Bus shelters & telephone booths in Ireland were wonderful homes, as were a pair of shoes, especially if they didn't leak, but come now I'm beginning to get nostalgic. A tread on an elevator can be home, albeit fleetingly. A table makes a very good home, though not in a restaurant generally. I mean the desk kind of table. A place in line at the bank can be quite homey. I find it possible to go to work as long as I can duck home every now & again. My daughters think I have a weak bladder but it's not that. I think home may very well be a certain amount of space & silence around my very own self. I slot myself into it whenever possible. Stationary slots work best though a car is an excellent home, even at full tilt.

I Am The Conqueror

I got a bit of good news today so I celebrated with a stint of grading. Champagne would have been nice. But grading's good too. Paper's like truffles. Grading has nose. I tried to jam it into a flute but it wouldn't fit. Damned near broke the glass. But it was a trip. First 7 or 8 papers were all fizz. Then things started to swing. As, Bs, & Cs rained down like hail, running to their command posts, taking no prisoners, adamant & steely-eyed. Papers that used to take 35 minutes to slog through were like butter in my hands. Even the little minuses gleamed. Comments arrived with the inevitability of a coat released from the pristine fingers of a bespoke tailor onto the shoulders of a very rich man—the total *aptness* of the ballooning parachute after gargantuan free-fall. *Sparkling! Brilliant! Crystalline! Flawless, precise structure! Suave attack! I was moved by such beauty! Very lovely finish! Elegant on the palate, precise & with chiseled tannins!* I had gotten into the zone. My jaws rattled. I was a grading machine. One long slipper of muscle. Pulsing. Ecstatic. I had risen above it all. A trapdoor opened in the sky & heaven sucked me in. Far below I could see my laboring form, shoulders hunched, tongue curled at lips' corner, fingers clenched, sweatily pushing the pen.

I Cast My Vote

I don't have a carriage & it's not Sunday but I ride up the hill in my Sunday-best.

I don't have a boat & Carleton Street is not water but I sail up the street.

It is evening. I am exhausted with that true American exhaustion.

I sail to the Fire Station to cast my vote.

The representative outside is like representatives everywhere. He's the one in the warm coat.

Inside the Fire Station it is practically hairy. There are practically puddles on the floor. A woman at a table shouts out to me to close the door.

It is my first time to vote.

Back outside, the representative stretches towards me only vaguely, and only with a murmur and not fingers. But I have all my pride about me like a warm coat.

When we get home, my daughter looks at pictures of polling booths in the literature and says: *We should have gone to one like that! A shiny one.*

We don't have freedom, I told her earlier, *we have freerdom.*

I Went To The Doctor

I went to the doctor. It had been so long since I'd seen a doctor I thought she was trying to interview me. When we first met, she said: *Married, Single, Widowed, Divorced?* I thought that was a bit much. But I told her about my children, my husbands, my job, my furnace, my fall. About how I slept like a top. And Gold's Gym. And the sunken garden in the Pendleton House which is a house inside a museum. And my famous story of how I immigrated 11 years ago with $400 and a 7-year old child. We talked about poetry. Well, duh. But it was actually much broader than most poetry interviews, looser yet more intense. She asked me about drug use. *Marijuana? Cocaine?* That made me laugh. Everyone was so interested in me. It was marvelous. Even the nurse in Reception asked as she was passing: *Do you happen to know your height?* Boy did I! Then the Office Manager arranged all my appointments. I haven't had so much attention since the MLA or my first wedding. I'm going back.

I Went To The Gym

I went to the gym Wednesday. It was a lot of fun. On the treadmill I couldn't help thinking of Oscar Wilde. I'd never been to a gym before. You have to laugh: all of us there putting in a lot of effort and going nowhere. Gym clothes are great. Just by putting them on you get slimmer, tougher, more resilient, more *salmon-like*. They act like some sort of massage. I guess the fabric has a built in toner. More like a fan-belt than clothes. I haven't been to the gym for almost a week but I feel great. Now when I go out I put on my gym clothes. It's not just a matter of sidling down to Walgreens to get something. Or strolling around in flip-flops. Now I have gym shoes & gym shirts & gym pants (not gym shorts though, I know my limits). When I go out I can't help springing up on people's lawns & doing maneuvers & feints & dancing in place. I can't help bopping around. Flip-flops keep you grounded and that's good, that's humble. But gym shoes send you hurtling out into the world like a coiled spring like blistering latex. It's an adjustment for sure, quite the identity-change.

We Went To The Moon

We went to the Moon. We wore puffy suits & boots. We had a lunar module.

We collected Moon rock. We bounced around. Later we had a roving vehicle.

Some people said it was a set-up. That it was done in a TV studio. That there should have been stars & the flag moved.

It was a long time ago now, forty years. We went back a few times but then we stopped. There was no atmosphere. The sky was black. Everything was there but it wasn't much.

When I saw the pale sketch of the moon in the sky this morning I remembered we went to the moon. Probably.

In The Woods

Last night I mailed a lot of heart-stamps to a lot of trees. It's sober in the forest—almost a stage set—nothing but huge, upwardly mobile trunks. It's like standing at arm's length among an at-ease army of headless & footless chests. With silence like a system of cups—like large acorn lids or coconut shells or even bodhráns—catching the large *thump-thump* (like the inside of a wardrobe) of the little red heart stamps knocking into the chests of the trees. And I standing, breathing, tacks clamped between my lips.

JED RASULA

So Jed Rasula dropped by & he was rapping about his Auntie Meggie who was a musher in the Iditarod I don't know how many times & actually took the Red Lantern in '95 after a whole saga of attempts to cross the Burled Arch of Nome. First try was in '78 & she scratched in Rohn. I mean she had barely left Wasilla. Okay she was a Rookie. Next time was '79, it would've been the southern trail but she scratched in Ophir citing a sick team and her leader did die. A double intussusception Jed said. In '80 she made it to Cripple. That was a northern year. 497 miles to Nome. Closing in. She had knee surgery in '82, something brewing since '79 Jed said, so she didn't get back on the trail till '85 when she scratched in Anvik. In '89—I guess maybe she had to had surgery on the other knee—she scratched in Grayling, citing a soft trail. 429 miles to go so she shaved 68 miles off her best to date. That was a southern year. Then finally—this is the killer—in '92 she scratches in Unalakleet citing a sore thumb. Only Shaktoolik, Koyuk, Elim, Golovin, White Mountain, and Safety to go, 229 miles Jed said. But she never gave up. It was incredible Jed said. She should've got the Most Improved Musher Award. But she got the Red Lantern in '95. No gold. Just a plaque. For stick-to-it-iveness. 17 days 6 hours 2 minutes & 5 seconds it took her, Jed said. In the Iditarod you know there's a lot of money at stake. In XXXIII the top 30 shared $705,000, with Robert Sorlie alone taking $72,067. There were 7 females, with

Jessie Royer, DeeDee Jonrowe & Aliy Zirkle in 9th, 10th, and 11th place, Jessica Hendricks 15th, Melanie Gould 23rd, Diana Moroney 27th and Harmony Barron 29th. By the time you get to 29th you're talking only $2,193. But Jessie Royer got $35,511 and DeeDee walked away with $29,244. DeeDee finished in 9 days 8 hours 49 minutes & 42 seconds in '98. And 9 days 11 hours 24 minutes and 7 seconds in '95. That's fast. Sorlie's not that fast. Auntie Meggie was a sport, Jed said. It wasn't about the money. But she had a dog that later won the Lolly Medley Golden Harness Award. That's like the Yale Younger for dogs. We were enthralled listening. Jed said Meggie's achievement was remarkable, exemplary, significant, instructive, and singular, while not without precedent. Where is she now we all wondered. Dead Jed said.

Life Is Too Easy

Saturday comes round & you clean your house. What could be easier. Everything you put out of place during the week you put back in place. You throw stuff out. You squirt *Spick'n Span* and *Murphy's Oil Soap*. As soon as you put everything back it starts moving out again so you'll have something to do next Saturday. It's all very fine. Your teeth crumble & you stop what you're doing & make an appointment to go to the dentist & the dentist shores them up & you're all set. Your gums wear out & you go to the periodontist & the periodontist nicks a piece of gum from here *voila* & sews it in there *voila* & *lo* bob's your uncle you're good as new though a bit frankensteinish & off you go. You haul stuff in & you haul stuff out. You go to work. You come home. Then it's Saturday again & you clean your house. There is no earthquake in your city & your parents or your children don't disappear. You are not 14 & about to be married off to a cousin who will beat you. You are not *a 2-year old girl carrying water*. You have not *been sad for 20 years*. You do not think of setting fire to yourself. Life is too easy to say anything further about it here.

Low Visibility Vehicles

Low visibility cars whizz along like transparent balloons pulled by a big child somewhere underground with asphalt-piercing string like a steel barb or laser or one of those remote control boxes with a stiff aerial. Like bubble-cars but definitely more bubble than car. While being all car. Low visibility cars are a new concept in urban transport. They're *fast*. They're *light*. They're *scary!* They're scary for other cars. They shoot out without warning. They loom. They spring. Empty streets cough them up like throat-stuck boiled sweets. There's no way of knowing a low visibility vehicle is coming. *It's here!* They're scary for you too. *You're the driver!* Hope you're wearing your air-bag suit. Hope you're the Michelin Man. Hope you got your mitts soldered to the wheel & your jaw wired. *Yeah!* Not for pussies.

Metaphor Recoil

A hunter examines a block of text. It is nothing like a poem. Though there are similarities. And differences. It is nothing like an elephant. Or a raccoon. Though certainly there are similarities. And differences. The hunter looks squarely at the text & thinks: *Now where can I get me a square cauldron to boil up some chow?* In the wake of that question comes a silence, a whoosh of wind, a rustle of leaves, a sudden darkening of the sky. The hunter is also a poet—and is afraid.

MUSIC

I love music.

I love music so much that sometimes when I'm listening to music in my car a whole tide washes over me & I think *My GOD!!! I GOTTA have some MUSIC!*

I reach out to turn the music on & find: It's already on.

News

I have adopted a 49-year old woman. I've always wanted to adopt. Of course I was thinking of a younger child. But by the time I got round to it this was all they had left. It's okay though. She's not as cute perhaps but there are major advantages to the older adoptee. For example, no diaper involvement. Not yet anyhow. Babysitting's not a problem. In fact, my new daughter could easily babysit my birth-daughter, who is nine. (That's not why I got her, of course). She doesn't make noise when she cries. She's quite independent. She can drive. She's got a job. I guess it would be easy to exploit such a child. I'm going to call her Gloria Mundi Terra Fundi the Fourth. GMTFF for short. It's pronounced Gimtif. And I'm going to love her. Yes I yam! *I yam I yam I yam!* I yam amn't I??? *Brrrrrrrrrrrr.* Who's Mama's little buh-buh-buh-buh-bubba! *Hhhhrrrrrrrrrrrrrrrr!*

Nordic China

My neighbor broke up with his wife & went to China. It was very sudden. He went to the northern part, Nordic China, where all the people are blonde. I saw a documentary about it once. All the girls looked like Brigitte Bardot. Except with straight hair & bangs. Green eyes. It's not a colonization thing apparently. Some sort of genetic throw-back. Actually Jason is blonde too, except with curly hair. I think it was a bit abrupt, him leaving like that. Even if things wouldn't work out, there's stuff to settle. Psychologically too. The funny thing is—his wife is Chinese. Not from the Nordic part though. Actually Tulsa. But you know what I mean.

ON BEING A WRITER

As a writer I have faced many struggles in life. Just last week—and for several months in fact—the mouse on my old laptop has been broken. I have to use a plug-in mouse. Even that's not working. The *s* key on my other laptop has fallen off. Working under these conditions is hell on earth. You need to keep your nerve. Today out in the field the mouse gave up the ghost. I had to open her up—without morphine or instruments. It was as if I was following instructions from above, or some deep race memory. In a matter of minutes the track ball & ring were on the table, my fingers as deep inside that mouse as stubby fingers can go inside something very small. I didn't have tweezers & had to hook the compacted dust from the little wheels with my fingernails. I sewed her up and got her ticking for a while. Some day soon I'm going to have to bring the laptop with the dodgy *s* key in to our guys in OIT. Now that scares me. It's been a while since I talked to anyone. And some day soon I'll have to bring my old rhinoceros in. You need courage in this line of work. Guts. Purpose. Savvy. The writing life is hard but you can't beat it if you've got the bug.

PARKING

Only recently has it occurred to me to park near where I'm going to go. If I'm going to the park park near the park. If I'm going to school park near school. If I'm going to the store park in the store parking lot. Until recently, I did things differently. To be fair, if I was going to the park I parked near the park because there is a long stretch of street by the park where it is easy to park. But if I was going to school I also parked near the park. And walked to school. In winter this could be tough. And winter is 7/12 of the year here. Do the figures. Yesterday I went to the Athenaeum which is a small private library in Providence. I was going to park near the park & walk but then I said *No, why don't I try the Athenaeum parking lot.* The Athenaeum parking lot is somewhere I've been—walking. There are four parking spaces & they are extremely narrow. I wrote a poem about them once. So yesterday I parked in the lot & *ran into* the Athenaeum & *picked up* a few DVDs. I felt so Audrey Hepburn, so much mistress of this my city of Providence. *And P.S.* The store parking lot example above was just a joke. I knew from early on that the store parking lot was the best place to park when going to the store. If you look at a store you will often notice a lot of cars out front & an obvious main place to go, i.e., the store. Before I could drive I walked to the store & winding my way through the cars out front often thought *Some day I'll park my car here.*

Personal Insurance

These are unpredictable times. I got a call from a man at dinner-time who wanted to sell me home security. I was not polite to him. He started to talk about murder. He said, *I know where you live.* It got me thinking. I've seen movies about guys like this. I feel I'm prepared. I take care to keep a fresh copy of myself in my closet at all times. I back up my files. If anything happens to me there will be another Mairéad to look after my children. That's the least I can do. I just can't believe some parents. They don't seem to realize the consequences of sudden death on a family. I mean, you could lose your house. The children would have nowhere to live. They would be split up. Everything would change, even the cat. And what do you do with a little black cat in the event of the death of the mortgage-holder? Send a piece of the cat here, a piece there? No matter which way you look at it, the cat would lose out, or at the very least go through a difficult period of adjustment. And I know all about them. I'm a single parent. I have to think about these things. My dream is to have a whole rack of Mairéads back to back in my closet. Some people might say it's extravagant but I see it as an investment. What can you do when you have children. It's about peace of mind.

POETIC JUSTICE

Of course the big thing these days is invisibility implants. Invisibility is a misnomer though. They don't actually make you invisible. Sort of a blur. Well, not a blur. Not like Robin Williams in that movie. Not out of focus. Your outline is still there, available for pleasantries, and you take up the same space etc as before. It's just that there's no depth to you. People can't tangle with you & you can't tangle with them. It's a security thing. Genius. Much better than house arrest or those ankle bracelets or that gadget beside the phone. The implant lets you go about your business, take care of yourself, etc. It's just that you can't mix or mingle. Nobody notices you. I've had it done. The weird thing is I can't remember why. These days if you get the implant you get an erase chip too. The memory's gone. But I must have done something. You don't just get sentenced to implants & chips for nothing. It's kinda lonely, I grant you that. But who am I to complain. I mean I could be behind bars, right. Plenty of people are. At least I can go out & about even if I can't exactly make contact.

Quick Movie

I had to watch the movie very fast because I was going out. The valedictorian. The guy. His sister. Her father. Inexplicable love. The break-up. Jail-time. On a plane to England. *Good movie!* Last night when I had more time I watched a Disney movie about an ice-skater who gave up a career in physics & broke her mother's heart. Everything came out okay in the end but I cried buckets. Tonight I didn't have time to cry. Anyway the physicist in tonight's movie took the fellowship.

Revision

The dogs in my neighbors' backyard have no way to process misery. We do. The dogs, stretched out in the dusty yard, might feel the sun steal along their broad pelts, slipping like quicksilver between the radiant hairs, & if sufficient pleasure is packed, might even, who knows, heave to their feet, swaying in hazy dance. But whatever about delight, I don't know that they can use pain for anything other than what my neighbors intend, i.e., attack. They do not think: *I will make something of this endless experience of lovelessness, confinement, & exposure to the elements. I will write a crown of sonnets.* Or *We will sing a duet.* But still, when these streets are rocked by sirens, as they daily are. When children shudder in their coops. When ambulances, those great can-openers of sound, slice up our street, I hear the dogs next door—or one of them—come to the chain-link fence & howl in mimicry, matching the siren's wail with fleshy tongue & throat & vocal chords, laying an answering salve, or question, over chaos.

Rose-Colored Spectacles

Every now and then I check in my rose-colored spectacles to test the rougher selvedges of life. Yesterday I went for a walk a little out of my neighborhood. I was scared. A very mean-faced white pimp pulled his car across the sidewalk in front of me. He wanted to talk but I kept going. Something about his demeanor suggested rabid dog. There was a power outage when I got home. Back out on my street I could hear the tortured screams of a child, high, recurrent, the same frantic notes played over and over. After the lights went back on there was a powerful smell of skunk. Whole neighborhoods crumble when I take off my spectacles. My own face crumbles, the kitchen floor, memory. Small clear patches loom out of the fog. Reality can be the closest imaginable thing to *delirium tremens*. Come to think of it, another name for *rose-colored spectacles* is *car*.

Shingle

The shingles on my house are grey & very like a whale except perhaps in that each one is small & flat rather than huge & relatively round. My house in general is more like a whale being huge & the sky around being quite like the ocean except in that it is not wet. Yet the motion & profundity of the ocean are somehow echoed in the stillness & distance of the sky. It is water-color rather than water & the clouds move across it like whales, carrying their houses on their backs.

Slippage

A researcher moved into the 19th century. It was not intentional. It started slowly in the cold archives room, maybe even because of the temperature and holding the body still. Her spirit seeped out, like honey, like light, and fed slowly into—or imperceptibly rained down like pollen or pixels or dots in a newspaper picture onto—the materials spread out on their folders on the table spread over her knees, and gradually an image was formed—her image—two-dimensional, in the new place. Her body worked on, propping its chin on its hands, its head drooping like a tired flower over her papers, shoulder-blades anxious, belly stashed between the bulwarks of elbows & thighs. In the 19th century she could be very quiet, quieter even than in the Rare Books Room. She carried letters between people who barely acknowledged her presence; she examined their buttonholes, frayed edge of a waistcoat, hand white as paper, curl of steam above a tea-cup held in a plain hand or adrift among a mess of papers in a drawing-room which should have seemed more strange. She came to their call, harked to their merriment, the senseless jocularity of voices long gone, it has to be said. She accompanied them in their most private moments, even to the hour of their death—the date of which she knew though they did not. She was virtuous in the 19th century, humble, with slippered feet, replete with knowledge and proud that though not rich or brilliant at least she was alive. Here, in the 21st century, she was quiet too. Quieter than before, her spirit elsewhere.

STATE PATHOLOGIST

I think she had rings. A black lacy bodice. Her bare arms round & small. Pale freckled skin suggestive of red hair. Though her hair is blonde, her expression intent. Her left hand, cool & precise, turns over the chocolate brown slabs of flesh, lifting its folds, her right hand taking notes. This is a woman's body, animated by expertise. The man, in his dying throes, is pinned by the surrounding crowd. He feels their hot pressure, their hunger for his life. They are winding it out of him on their spindles. He drowns in his own breath, his panting opening a tunnel through them. He sees the watery bog, golden reeds, whipped cotton, tattoo of tiny blue flowers, the massive overwhelming sky. Sluices his last draught of pain & is resurrected—2,500 years later— into her hands.

THAT *WEST END BLUES* SYNDROME

What is that *West End Blues* syndrome? You know, when someone says *Ooh West End Blues ooh* & wags their head in disbelief at a total loss for words. *Oooh West End Blues* & then just—aposiopesis. What makes *West End Blues* something that say *Beau Koo Jack* is not? You don't hear people saying *Oooh that Beau Koo Jack*. And *Beau Koo Jack* is a pretty good tune with wild bits. So what is it? What makes *West End Blues* magnificent? It's not that I don't recognize the syndrome. Like you write thousands of "poems" & suddenly—*jackpot!* You got a classic. You recognize it instantly or certainly within a few years & others recognize it too just as quick. You're absolutely thrilled to have produced a classic & don't know how you did it & but *you did it you did it you did it Hallelujah Lord!* But how does the classic thing happen? Why this & not that? Why then & not now? Why him & not me? What gives that *West End Blues* a free march into your soul? So yes you have that opening horn carving a staircase in the sky. Then the slow jog oh yes with the comfy undertow & the cornucopia of promises above & the tease of horn & lulling swing & knocking of the little clappers like Rudolph clip-clopping on the first day of summer. It's quite a stroll. Then some slight complaining from the trombone, some insinuation & suggestion, well isn't that just the way. Then that musy clarinet & Louis's sympathetic wad-wad-wa wad-wad-wadda. With the piano marking time oh yes no argument. Then enter Earl for sure with featherlight fingering. Tinkle

& thump & trill. The delicious stir-up of it all presided over by that long slow horn arching out & out & out & out. Louis ever so delicate inserting himself to string his tightrope between skyscrapers & pick his way across into the desultory dissolution of the small hours, well it has to happen the dawn. Then Zutty's woodblock click. Oh yes that's something. But what? That is my point here people. And *hey* fyi did you ever wonder what the W.E.B. in Du Bois stood for? You got it.

The Important Looking Men

The important looking men are not always the important looking men. Sometimes the important looking men are women. Sometimes the important looking men are the woman with the brown helmet of hair, head tilted attentively. Sometimes the important looking men are not the important looking men but visitors from out-of-town where they are not important either. The tortured artist is not always the tortured artist. The tortured artist is not always the guy in the thin cardigan smoking a cigarette outside the studio. That might be the electrician. The tortured artist is sometimes the small priest who stands in the corner of the salon balancing his cup of tea. Or the woman nobody sees. The lover is not always the lover. The lover can be a liar, refracting images of himself back into infinity. The lover might be this beagle, this couch, this slipper, this child who shouts out to me this morning late for school—tumbling from his father's car & again from the side-walk—*Clio's Mom!* Or this other child, this evening, alone, walking home, who tosses his glorious *hello* across Camp Street to land at my feet.

The Letter

The letter was urgent so I wrote it inside the envelope. It was awkward. If I could've stood inside the envelope in white coveralls reaching up to write with my giant brush on the great billboard of the page I would've. If I could've swung from a cradle to write it I would've. I would've whistled. But as it was I had to crookedly insert my pen into the strained envelope & blindly write. The letter was about ballet slippers: *Dear Fest Ball. My daughter. Prob with ballet slippers. Not told. Felt bad. Target Payless no good. Minor surgery. Very happy. Sad again. Target Payless Wal-Mart. Loan of used slippers. Washed well. Not a match. One too small tight. Lot of money. I feel 3 sessions. Likes to jump. If safety. Doing best. But Friday. Dance in socks. Sincerely.* In a sense it was a holding letter. A place-holder. Almost a substitute. My daughter, holding the finished letter (slightly twisted), was also holding the slippers, their blunt snouts dreaming inside their dim sac. The envelope was a type of shoe-bag. A skein into which the missing slippers were slung. She could almost wear them surely or be said to be wearing them, as she danced across the painted floor of the studio, barely visible paper slippers sheathing her abashed feet.

The New Sponge

The new sponge has somehow become the old sponge. It seems only the other day I bought it though I can't remember a thing about that day anymore than I'll remember a thing about today tomorrow. I have it in front of me in a baggie. On one side it is pink plastic mesh with blue blanket stitching around the edges. It looks semi-okay though grimy. Captured in the slightly billowing baggie, it looks like a metaphor for something edible, e.g., a very flat small burrito made of *Twizzlers*. It could also be a cordon of police trying to contain a desperate crowd beneath a collapsing sports dome, or even just a televised version of something like that. The baggie itself is majestic. A cross between an amniotic sac & a cathedral. It makes the sponge (actually a scrubbie) look like an extra-terrestrial bride in alien *haute couture* more than food. On the reverse side, however: a different story. The bubbled sponge is slashed viciously from right temple to left chin almost, its stunned face torn by a gaping wound oozing dirty pancake batter (half-done), with a suggestion also of the head on a very old pint of Guinness or the foam stuffing in cheap furniture, the crusty kind. The contrast between the ghastly violated blue sponge & the still somehow upright blue blanket stitching is sickening. Even the baggie seems to want to get away. What happens if I ditch them both together, bound in distasteful partnership, the scrubbie incarcerated forever in ghostly plastic, in a sense buried alive? Well, whatever. There are other things to write about. Surely.

The Olden Days

In the old days, shoes had hems. People could do everything in those days: build boats, grow food, make stakes for beanstalks, weave cloth, wear fustian, skin deer, gut fish, make home remedies—and all their own clothes & shoes. Boots needed a hem. People had a lot of children & children grew fast. When the child grew you let the hem out, just like clothes except that with clothes you let the hem down not out. Things weren't disposable like they are now. If you made a pair of shoes you wanted them to last. So kids grow. And by & large you want them to. But shoes take time. You couldn't be making them every year or 6 months. Especially if you had 8 or 10 kids. Sure you'd be at it year-round. In time though people lost the knack for making hems. The generation gap set in. People weren't so quick to pass the knowledge on. The secret got lost. If people had 8 or 10 children, they started to say, well Tommy can wear Betty's boots, Betty can wear Alfonse's, Al can wear Joe's, Joe can wear Eileen's, Eileen can wear Angelica's, Angelica can wear Dicky's, Dicky can wear Rose's, Rose can wear Freddy's, Freddy can wear Twit's, Twit can wear Ebenezer's, and we'll get new boots for Ebenezer, he's nine. This was the beginning of all sorts of gender dysporia, alienation, & social unease, not to mention veruccas. No-one felt right in their shoes. It was a very different feeling from the old days, when you could let the hem out & stay in the groove of your very own pair of shoes all the way up through childhood. It's amazing how the most minute changes in domestic economy can affect a culture. People nowadays have never heard the word *husbandry*. That scares me. People think *more more*. When in fact all that is needed is to extend the thing that is there.

The Pressure

This evening I cleaned the fridge. The pressure. You know when you have all the milk cartons out. Oh! I know it's November. But unseasonably warm right. The pressure. The pressure. It was horrendous. It was hellish. I went at it like the devil. Like a giant *Energizer* bunny. *Brrrrrrrrrrrrrrrrrrrrrrrrrr!* My attack was kinda like a sander, kinda like a drill, kinda like a chainsaw. *Out, out, everything out! Hands over heads! Put down your weapons!! Lay your weapons down!!!!* A jar of *Newman's Own* (garlic & peppers) tried to hide out at the back—sorta like the ending of *Butch Cassidy*—but we forked it out, along with a colony of yogurt occupying the zone. Rooted them out screaming. Brie! Ham! Pickles! You name it. Things crawling everywhere, trying to burrow in the corners or the crisper. There was a hardened Parmesan hanging onto the door. You're never too old to fight. Then there they were— all huddled on the counter-top. What a crew. Half of them rotten. Scared. Some of them just kids. But still: past their sell-by date. In some cases grievously past. They had to go. Over the top. One after another—I had lined up the garbage can—*GO! GO! GO!* Have you ever seen a pint of half-and-half quaking, man? How about 3 chocolate macaroons? They were *white!* [CLEARS THROAT] Sure, there were items I felt sorry for. I'm human. I felt sick for them. But that's life. It's *Thanksgiving*, man. We're moving the new guys in.

The Russian Week

Inside this week is another week & inside that week is another week & inside that week is another week & inside that week is another week & inside that week is another week & inside that week is another week so that instead of 7 days each week is actually composed of 7 weeks each one a little smaller than its container week but still workable & with rosy cheeks. This arrangement is necessary. If a week were only a week *aka* a standard 7-day week it would not be possible to get things done. Therefore *voila*: The Russian Week. As soon as it becomes apparent that everything cannot get done in the albeit larger, more commodious week, one can simply crack open the inside week, only slightly less commodious in size. Then, when things pile up as they are wont to do, one proceeds to the inside-inside week, its size only slightly less commodious again. And so it goes. I will not go through the process in tedious detail. For that it would be necessary to have an inside-inside-inside-inside-inside-inside-inside week, i.e., 8 weeks in all and obviously that is impossible. There may be some future in developing a system whereby each of the 7 weeks which constitute the week would in turn contain 7 weeks, giving 49 weeks in all inside one week, and indeed the prospect of an *ad infinitum* progression. But this proposal lacks the calm symmetry of the established model. It is knobby & hectic where the other is smooth, rounded, generous, economical—and natural. Thank God for the Russian week.

The Tired Terrorist

The terrorist was tired. *Goddammit* he said, *I could do with some bacon & eggs.* He was sick to the back teeth of killing. It was ugly. He'd had enough. He laid down his shotgun, his nail-bomb, his knife. He emptied his pockets. He unzipped his jacket. He thought of the spare room in his mother's house. What he wouldn't give to be under the peach coverlet right now, morning radio barely audible, shouts of the children outside, the smell of bacon wafting up the stairs. Or more foreign breakfasts. Croissants & apricot jam. Fresh bread & honey. Watermelon. Yogurt. Smoked horse. Even noodles.

THE WIND THAT SHAKES THE BARLEY

My mother sits inside me like a frog. We are watching a movie. It is *The Wind That Shakes the Barley*. At first I think my mother will like it but then I realize she will not. It is dark in the movie theatre, so dark it seems empty. I am crouched down in my seat & my mother is crouched down in me. On the screen terrible things are happening. Micheál is battered to a pulp for saying his name in Irish. His insides are smeared all over him. The Black & Tans jump their rifle butts into men's faces breaking their noses & teeth. They are panic turned lethal. An octopus of shout. They hack off a girl's hair taking great swipes of her scalp. The Black & Tan captain draws Teddy's fingernails out with a rusty pliers. The Black & Tans kill the boys. The boys kill the Black & Tans. Then the boys kill each other. *The old story we all know we know it so well.* Though it is not spoken about. It is like heavy metals in our bones. We are made of its secrets. My mother is stirring inside me, anxious to eat.

Third Hand

What's the good of washing your hands in order to eat when then you have to handle money in order to get the food? What can be more unsanitary than money? If you're alone you can't put your tray on the table & scoot to the bathroom to wash your hands. The restrooms might be floors away. Your food would be cold or gone. And anyway you have to touch doors & handles & all sorts of things on the way back. Even if you sort of push the doors with the long side of your forearm, not all doors open like that. And what about elevator buttons? You can't do it with your nose. No. What you need is a third hand. This third hand would be the hand you'd use to push doors or elevator buttons or pay money to the cashier. The Arabs have it half right. But it's too late for Westerners to adapt. We're used to using both hands in the eating—and washing—process. A credit card is a type of American third hand. It stays mostly in the wallet or pocket-book and being glossy doesn't pick up outrageous germs. Still it's a teeny-weeny bit more interactive than I can be totally comfortable with. It passes from hand to hand, and promiscuously through machines. Do you remember the first time you heard the word *swipe*? I do. Anyway back to the third hand. So—how to set about getting this baby together. Pointers people?

Three Irish Poets

Editors of anthologies & special features on Irish poetry take note: I am available for inclusion in such publications in 3 guises: Irish Woman Poet, Innovative Irish Poet and, as the field is currently wide open, Ireland's First Concrete Poet.* I can furnish a complete set of poems for each identity, in addition to sensitively selected yet pronounceable names: Minnie O'Donnell, Irish Woman Poet; Clare Macken, Innovative Irish Poet; and Bo Doyle-Hund, Ireland's First Concrete Poet. Sample available sets include: "My Transistor Radio," "Léim an Bhradáin," "Rites of Passage" (Minnie O'Donnell); "Trans/is/t," "Apostrophe for Finnegan," "Electoral Capacity" (Clare Macken); and "ciúnas," "'," and "18" (Bo Doyle-Hund). I am working on a fourth identity—"A Remarkable Poet in Her Own Right." The tentative title for this character is: "Mairéad Byrne."

*No further jokes about building sites please.

Traditional Pot

When I got married my mother gave me the traditional pot. From that time on everything I cooked was cooked in the traditional pot. And I mean everything. The first Christmas was such fun. On "Brides' Day" in January I met with all the other new brides in the family to tell stories about how we managed Christmas dinner. It was a laugh. Of course my husband that year was an actuary & he had drawn graphs & flow charts, all sorts of mappings & schedules & sequences to cook the mushrooms & turkey & potatoes & stuffing & celery & tomatoes & zucchini & all the trimmings & sauce. In & out of the pot. It was the very devil trying to keep things hot. And then the mince pies & plum pudding & cake! Thank God for sherry trifle is what I say! It was insane. Not for nothing did us girls breast-feed our babies until they were big enough for school lunches! Well husbands come & go as we know but the traditional pot stays on its sacred burner until the oldest daughter marries & leaves home. For that day believe me I have plans.

Trapeze Act

Under this house, ladies and gentlemen, underneath this 4-story house, you do not see a safety net. There is no safety net beneath this house. You can pass your hands under—*see*—nothing! We have a woman ascending a white staircase. Beneath her feet, treads. The staircase is hollow. It rests on wide planks. Struts. Air. A skim of cement. Dirt. The house falls away. She sits on the top step, soft-angled, listening. We can lift her from room to room—look! Her children are curled in their beds. No-one holds this house in his cupped palm. This house hangs like a hive from a bough. Tilting. Plummeting.

Washing My Keys

It's Saturday & it's lashing raining so I'm staying home washing my keys. Not enough people think to do this. But look what your keys do for you. They can be like your best friend. A comforting weight in your pocket. Cool metal in the palm of your hand. The *open sesame* to your familiar world. It's not just a matter of hygiene though it is that too (I mean what do your keys *do* in there?)—it's a matter of *tending to*. I always start with my car key. It's the biggest on the bunch. I have a nice little pastry brush for that. *Flick flick.* My car key looks sort of unfinished but I know that's just the look. It's casual. Like how the car starts. A hiccup. A purr. Then action. Next comes my little *Master* locker key. This is a really small key so I use a little carbon nanotube brush with bristles so tiny a thousand of them could fit inside a strand of hair. It so happens that my car key & my *Master* locker key are side-by-side on my ring. Really I should re-arrange my keys in order of size, either descending or ascending. It's not nice to have jolts. The thing is, you need different tools to clean each one. A boar bristle pastry brush with blue ferrule & long bristles works well with the car key but I don't like laying it down on my instrument table next to an almost invisible nanoparticle brush actually small enough to clean up unwanted deposits in arteries & other blood vessels. There's something incongruous about that. I'd much rather have a logic to the thing. Lay the tools on the slab in order of size too. Then I could be as precise as a surgeon. Maybe even have an assistant to hand me stuff: *Now I'll have the Polenov Male Tail Kolinsky Brush please Nurse. Hmm. Feather Pastry Brush with Bunched Goosed Feathers please. Yes, and the 1" Round China Bristle, Lorna.* Pretty soon I'd be abbreviating: *Feather. Male Tail. 1" Round.* We'd have an intuitive rhythm. *Thank you Nurse. Nice job peeps.* Though it's as much like a manicure as surgery. Extending each key like a bony finger through the bars in *Hansel & Gretel.* Anyway I don't want to get hung up on extremes. The bulk of keys on my ring are mid-size: a secret key; LA office key; another secret key; 59BB; duplicate LA office key; a silver key to all the inside doors in my house; office key; house key. There's also store cards: *Petco, Blockbuster, CVS, Stop'n Shop.* I give them all special attention & then a good overall *rub-a-dub-dub.* I have lovely rinsy stuff to wash the bubbles away. Then a nice bit of flannel & *chamois* for shine. Pretty soon I'll be sending away for a special outfit to wear when I'm washing my keys. If you do a job do it right I say. In the old days we would stick keys in a bowl of sand to clean them. Not anymore. I'm in America now.

Watches Are Kinda Like Chips

Watches are kinda like chips, except you wear them on the outside, voluntarily. They're not embedded. They're not implants. But they have a similar surveillance feel to them, if you know what I mean. First off, watches feel like they were strapped on. I mean strapped on by someone who is not you. Some huge thug who had to kneel on your chest to get enough leverage while you were so much putty beneath his hands. You might have been asleep. Then you wake up & feel something kinda flat & heavy on your wrist. You crank your head around and—oh, it's just your watch. And then you spend the rest of the day looking at it. You practically beg its permission to go to bed at night. And first thing next day there it is again. It's just a big cornflake of a chip basking on your wrist until its transit papers to the interior come through. Watches are also rites of passage. You're so ensconced in the culture that you take the pain, as in some forms of teenage circumcision & mutilation rituals. I mean how many people are going to have the vision to stand outside themselves & say: *Hey! What is that great big flat thing on my wrist? I mean what IS that??* It's like watches are both anthropological *and* futuristic. They're a sort of primitive chip, a little clunky but good enough until they get round to something more svelte, like kangaroo pouches are a good start but not quite the condos *el utero* provides.

We Had A Laugh

It was at Thanksgiving. We were watching a movie called *The Lake House*. Sandra Bullock went into a bar & ordered a drink. The barman plopped it down in front of her. My daughter said *What did she order?* I said *A glass of milk*. We nearly died laughing at that. At least I did. I don't know what condition my daughter was in. I couldn't see. My eyes were sealed shut. It was all dark. I felt very tight inside. I could feel the seams of my eyelids like a ridge. Laughs were chocking out of me like I was a Pez dispenser. My lips were stretched wide in a rictus—not like a *gape* or anything loose but like a bird's beak. My whole face was turning into a skull. I was laughing. I was happy. But it was kind of disturbing too. I wouldn't want anyone to see me laughing like that. I hoped my daughter was rolling around in her own pandemonium. Though a few weeks ago a fit of laughter overtook me in Thayer Street. I was falling against walls & lurching into stores until my daughter plucked me back by the nape. Anyway at Thanksgiving we had a laugh. Another funny bit was when Sandra Bullock's fiancé was sitting at a desk in the other room behind a giant laptop. I said *Whoa look at the size of his laptop*. Then my daughter said *It's not a laptop. It's a desk-top.* That laugh became a great dark sack of its own too. I should get out more.

WHAT IS A CELL PHONE?

A cell phone is a kind of clock. You don't use it to check the time. Though of course you can. You use it to check that you exist. On the porch—*am I still here?* In the driveway—*Am I here?* In the car—*What about now, am I here?* At the intersection—*Oh golly strangers everywhere buses trucks Mama I'm turning keep talking for God's sake* yeah. You pat yourself down more efficiently than any arresting cop.

A cell phone is a mobile bed. A security blanket. Saran wrap for the Reichstag of your head.

Cell phones are a new dimension. They have revolutionized the concepts of out & in. You're never really out. Unless you're comatose. And when you're in, you're often out. You can be in your car, perched on your honey's knee, virtually. Or sullen on your couch, staring at your buzzing phone. Are you "in" or "out"? Impossible to tell. A cell phone offers many inexplicables, always in quotation marks.

A cell phone is a motor. You plug your loaf in & before you know it you have exchanged one set of familiar surroundings for another. A cell phone is a stun gun of the *in between* while simultaneously allowing no other state.

About The Author

Mairéad Byrne's previous publications include two poetry collections, *SOS Poetry* (/ubu Editions 2007), and *Nelson & The Huruburu Bird* (Wild Honey Press 2003); and three chapbooks, *An Educated Heart* (Palm Press 2005), *Vivas* (Wild Honey Press 2005), and *Kalends* (Belladonna* 2005). She  Photo: Marina Byrne-Folan

is an Associate Professor of English at Rhode Island School of Design in Providence. With Ian Davidson, she is the co-manager of the listserv British & Irish Poets. Before immigrating to the United States in 1994, she was a journalist, playwright, arts centre director, and teacher in Ireland.